THE

May this journey
bring you reflection,
inspiration and a will
to chase joy and present
living.

Malia Sperling

THIS IS JOY

A PATH TO FINDING JOY, GRATITUDE AND THE PRESENT

.

MALIA SPERLING

Notice

Publishing Services by Happy Self Publishing
www.happyselfpublishing.com

Illustrations created by Malia Sperling

Library of Congress

In dedication to the people in my gratitude journey:
You have taught me more than you will ever know.

Contents

ACKNOWLEDGMENTS

In truth, this collection of work belongs to the many people responsible for bringing me great joy in life. I wouldn't be the woman I am today if it weren't for their intentional influence. In life there are transcending moments that present themselves with great purpose and this book represents one of them for me. I am forever grateful for the many people and experiences that came together in an effort for this vision to come to life. As I have learned from this journey, everything is possible when intentional work is applied to an active adventure. This requires the willingness to feel vulnerable, curious, humble and daring. Real growth and life change are often the result of such happenings.

This experience has proven to me that a vacancy of surprise and delight exists in our daily lives. We live for certainty, scheduling and structure. Unfortunately, these things manifest stress, inflexibility and rigid routine. If it weren't for the surprise and delight of my husband's gratitude letter gifted to me on my 37th birthday, this beautiful, eye-opening adventure may never have existed. It is in the gift of surprise, deep delight and sincerity that true joy can be felt. He has been the source of my inspiration since the very beginning and through his gift my life will forever be changed. This journey showcases the importance of surprise, delight, exploration and adventure in life. In many ways, we are lost without it.

There are two people in my journey that are not only responsible for its beginning, but very intentional close to it in a meaningful way. Both my mother and stepfather were diagnosed with cancer within the same time frame of receiving my husband's letter and thus, kick-started my quest to send letters of gratitude. Over the course of that year, we began an intentional commitment to being present with each other. We spent time learning to say the things that needed to be said, devoting time to just talking and leaving nothing on the table. My mother beat the odds and pulled through miraculously, giving our family a renewed commitment to making memories together. My stepfather fought with a fierce passion for his life, a battle that spanned 18 months and ended with his closest family members by his side sharing final prayers and devotions of love. It was with every bit of confidence and conviction of the heart that I was able to say, "You know exactly how I feel about you. You know just how much you mean to me, and how much I love you. You know how blessed I am to have had you in my life, and I am happy knowing that God is ready to welcome you to heaven with open arms and love." I share this very personal sentiment in its entirety, because it is the truth. If it weren't for the timing of my husband's letter or my commitment to being present with my parents, I may have lost the opportunity to share the things I needed to say before it was too late. In a year that many would describe as sorrow filled, stressful and uncertain; the outcome of feeling extreme levels of joy and gratitude might seem out of place. An overwhelming sense of deep delight, love, gratitude and light poured through my soul as I reflected on this span of time. Proving to me that one must look beyond the circumstances of life and rather, zoom in on the opportunities that exist daily to be present with the people in our lives.

There have been hundreds of moments, epiphanies and exchanges throughout this experience with people that have forever altered the way in which I live my life for the better. A fierce passion for the present was born, and a commitment to creating joyful memories with family, friends and the people I interact with daily. The past year has been filled with adventure, laughter, travel and an abundance of meaningful conversation. Relationships with my husband, children, mom, brother, niece, nephew and dearest friends are among the many that have flourished.

This process has taught me that all is not lost. Anyone can make a change and completely transform the way in which he or she dedicates quality time to the people and experiences in life that matter most. It is the most refreshing starting point for anyone looking to get off the hamster wheel and reconnect with self and life priorities. Cal Jernigan, Lead Pastor of Central Christian Church, has been a true guiding light, inspiration and profound mentor in the creation of this process and is quoted at several points in my story. Additionally, no book would be complete without the talents of a great editor. Skyler Dillon has been a perfect match from the start, bringing life, depth and perspective to the journey. I am blessed to have worked with such a beautiful person and gifted editor.

With absolute certainty I can say that this was the most defining year of my life. It provided great clarity, purpose, perseverance and light. It is through my faith that I have grown exponentially as a person, learning to be more present, a better servant and more mindful of the people I am blessed to have in my life. Life requires continuous growth, granting us experiences that lead to transcending moments, opportunities and action. As you embark on your journey today; may you open your heart and mind, bare your soul, live in the present and look for intentional opportunities to serve others always. May you recognize that there is a light within you, capable of shining bright for all to see.

CHAPTER ONE

OVER THE RAINBOW: WHERE DREAMS BECOME REALITY

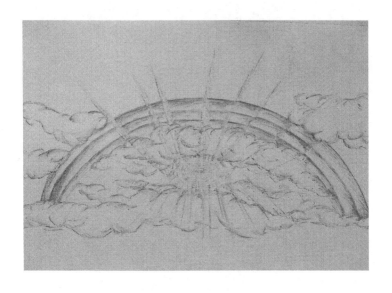

"Somewhere over the rainbow
Way up high.
There's a land that I heard of
Once in a lullaby.

Somewhere over the rainbow
Skies are blue.
And the dreams that you dare to dream
Really do come true.

Someday I'll wish upon a star
And wake up where the clouds are far
Behind me.

Where troubles melt like lemon drops
Way above the chimney tops
That's where you'll find me.

Somewhere over the rainbow
Bluebirds fly.
Birds fly over the rainbow.
Why then, oh why can't I?

If happy little bluebirds fly
Beyond the rainbow
Why, oh why can't I?"
(Arlen & Harburg, 1939).

— Harold Arlen and E.Y. Harburg

There are times in life when we are suspended in air, floating. We are going through the motions of what each day brings us, over and over again. Inside there is a yearning for more: more love, more success, more meaning, more adventure, more friendship, more excitement, more laughter, more significance, more faith, more, more and more.

We are waiting for something or someone to grab hold of our attention and compel us to take action. But how, when, or what will it be? What will *it* take?

It begins by opening our eyes and intentionally looking for the moments in life that present opportunity, clarity and a pathway to achieving something remarkable. Dorothy's journey in the land of OZ is the perfect example. It details the enchantment that is entirely possible when allowing one's self to step outside of the box and adventure down a new path. Like a hamster in a wheel, some of us are running at top speed, either to keep up or to escape the very realities that bring routine to our daily lives. Others are trapped, overwhelmed and caged by the walls that define them, simply unable to gather enough strength to make the change needed. So we wait: Wait for that tornado, strong and mighty and able to grab physical hold of our lives, shaking us upside, downside, right ways and left. As if plunged in a deep cool river, we surface with a new lens -- a lens that is in no way representative of the black and white gray tones we once looked upon, and features color so vivid, so bright, even our own eyes cannot believe. And that field of grass, oh so green, more beautiful than one could ever imagine! There it was, what we had been searching for all along: a world of color, wonder and possibility. A land of what ifs and if onlys, where troubles can melt like lemon drops and the dreams we wish can in fact come true. *The Wizard of Oz* motion picture brings life to fear and vulnerability through characters and images that only our wildest dreams could manufacture. This alone entraps our minds, emotions and imagination as we walk along the yellow brick road hand-in-hand with Dorothy, discovering with each step the fear that binds us, the light that frees us and the euphoria that we conjure as we experience deep levels of Joy. Over that beautiful rainbow, we experience the positive outcomes that can occur when fear is confronted, courage is found and gratitude is discovered. It is through the new found relationships with Scarecrow, Tin Man and Lion that Dorothy's quest for answers reveals the very reasons why the people in her life matter. This active adventure and vivid character portrayal reacquaint Dorothy with the love, compassion and adoration of the people she knows best - the people responsible for bringing the greatest Joy to her life.

Dreams give us the ability to see for a moment what our mind is capable of solving subconsciously. In our awake hours we become consumed and overwhelmed by the details in life that hinder us from taking action to solve problems or chase happiness. If this is true, then the answer of what waits beyond the rainbow has in fact been in the palm of our hands all along and the way to find that green grass is entirely up to where we water it.

> *"When you are grateful, fear disappears and abundance appears"* (Robbins).
> **– Anthony Robbins**

Today, I ask that you open your heart and mind as we journey together down a new path. With a little focus, discovery, courage and passion, "Everything is possible, even the impossible" (Mary Poppins Returns). Thanks to masterfully told stories, belief and wonder provide the inspiration needed to achieve what we may deem "the impossible." These dreams, though wild in our minds can certainly become real when effort translates to action. To begin we must start broad. Through reflection, the mind will begin to open and embrace what comes next.

Start by asking yourself these questions:

1. Have you ever taken a leap of faith and acted on something without knowing what may come of it?
2. Has the outcome of a goal or experience ever far exceeded your original expectations?
3. What actions in your life have attributed to real, everlasting change in a meaningful way for you and the people you care about most?

4. When was the last time you achieved a goal that had sizable impact on your life?

I am hopeful that you answered yes to some of the questions above, and that such occurrences continue to bless your life routinely. For some of us, the answers to these questions may be no, or not recently, and that's okay. As we age and progress through life, finding ways to make real, positive change with consistency over time can prove challenging. But I believe the process is worth the work. Some of these aspirations are critical for life itself. They demand a decision and effort. Others come wrapped up in self-improvement and betterment goals, ultimately adding personal growth and esteem to our lives. "These two types of Interpersonal goals, self–image goals and compassionate goals, reflect distinct motivational perspectives on the relationship between the self and others- egosystem and ecosystem perspectives, respectively" (Crocker, Oliver & Nuer, 2009). Self-worth and the concept of compassionate goals represent the high-value psychological needs we have as social beings. Here's what a force ranking of such goal categories might look like:

1. Sustaining life requirement: unpredictable and consequence heavy, requiring change
2. Self-image: something solely benefiting one's self
3. Compassionate: helps us measure our individual impact on others and the greater good

Sustaining life goals are those that we cannot predict or ignore. They can introduce themselves at any stage of life and they require swift response and effort. Disease, job loss or care giving are examples of such situations. They take precedence over any other conflicting priority. The other two forms of goals fall into two distinct interpersonal goal categories: Self-Image and Compassionate. There are obvious stages in life when self-image goals carry greater weight in value. One is in early adulthood as people are working to prove themselves worthy of the character they are selling. It is a heavy period of selling, for friendship, careers and romantic relationships. As life moves forward, a natural shift occurs from self-image to compassionate priorities. As social human beings, we require touch, love, thought and purpose through interaction with others. It is known to play a major role in physical and psychological wellness. The reciprocal nature of giving and receiving emotional support, inspiration and growth fulfills a deeper human need. You can see the fruits of these moments in the bonds that form through marriages, parenthood and close relationships with friends and family. Through compassion we learn that we must first give in an effort to preserve self-worth. "Self-image goals have costs for belonging, and compassionate goals have benefits for belonging" (Crocker, Oliver & Nuer, 2009).

We have much to give and purpose to bestow on the world. The world as we measure it is ours to change. The ways in which we influence are entirely up to us.

Our reach and impact are limitless and created by the legacy of what sits in our hearts and minds. As we move through life, the barriers that prevent us from committing to substantial life changing outcomes can seem impossible to overcome. Fear, lack of confidence, judgment, accountability, time, belief, strength, ability and daily distractions cloud our vision. We struggle with the opportunity cost or the loss of giving something up in its place. These life changing opportunities come in many shapes and sizes: diets, health, relationships, career, family, travel, church, volunteering, home and finally…happiness.

The key to committing to a goal of this magnitude is the evaluation of its outcome. Does the outcome outweigh the cost of making the life change? More importantly, is the outcome something that can be sustained and benefited from over time? This last statement is by far the greater make-or-break decision maker of the equation. Most of the heavy hitter life changing outcomes we chase will in fact require a baseline commitment and behavioral expectation for life once the plateau has been reached. If we are unwilling to commit to the sustaining efforts, we fall back to ground zero. Which is why, if we cannot quantify a large sustained benefit of maintaining a goal over time, we choose not to begin. The sad truth is that we give up the value of needed life change because we are unwilling to maintain it. Why, when this is the easiest part of all? Climbing the mountain is by far the most strenuous leg of the trip. The momentum you gain from basking in the glory of achievement at the mountain top is what feeds your hunger to continue the journey. Growth is a critical piece to our life's journey. You should never give yourself permission to stop growing. I am not speaking about New Year's resolutions or trendy fads, but real growth; transformational growth. Remember back to your childhood when "growth" was all that you could think about? Your days broke with a hearty passion for growth, including school, sport, friendship, skill, talent and possibility! And as intentionally as the day began, it ended with dreams, fantasies, plans and prayers centered on the future.

What transformational growth lies in front of you?

What anchors your mind throughout your day? And, what completes your final thought as you drift off to sleep?

Perhaps this is where the answer lies.

While our personal needs and aspirations are often unique and aspirations much like a Monet painting, they share common ground. It is here that transformational growth that will change our lives for the better, forever, can be achieved.

CHAPTER TWO

THE GIFT OF GRATITUDE: A QUEST FOR JOY THROUGH THE EXPRESSION OF GRATITUDE

ompassionate goals are some that pay the highest of dividends in return for action. They provide benefit to the psychological needs of human beings, yet exist at the lowest executable stage of goal setting. The societal shift from conversing face-to-face to communicating via text and social media has further driven compassionate priorities to extremes. The physical and psychological wellness of once strong, healthy and reciprocal relationships has been compromised, further highlighting the need for change. Good quality relationships shared with other human beings is a basic need for life wellness. It is a compassionate priority that can be easily addressed with some reasonable change and boasts magnificent returns.

There really is nothing in life that delivers such pure happiness than what we receive through the bond we have with the people in our lives. While this is one thing that many of us can agree on, the current status of such relationships is not always active, fruitful or present. This is not by fault; it is a cyclical condition of life. Like with a good book, we get sucked in, hooked by a common thread, lost in the emotion of the story unfolding and then, as if out of nowhere, it ends. We want to hold onto those last few chapters with every bit of strength we can muster up, re-reading key sentences until finally realizing that all good things must come to an end. Eventually, our attention is pulled elsewhere and that book we love oh so much gets placed on a shelf waiting to be called upon at a later time. We wouldn't dare give it away. We even stop to admire it, recall our favorite chapters and then safely store it back up on that shelf out of harm's way. Isn't this just like the pivotal relationships we hold in life? We are active at times, live dormant at others and treat the most sacred as life's greatest treasures. In a world of chaos, busy schedules, constant demands, expectations and communication styles that hinder relationship building, we long for the ability to restore Joy in the once present relationships of our lives.

How can it be done? How could we possibly move from here to there?

Is it possible to move surviving relationships to a state of thriving?

Can we improve communication and move back to a progressive form of being present with people?

If we could, what impact would this have on life?

Most great "aha" moments in life are experienced and discovered, not told. In fact, some of the very best are those that surprise the heck out of us! They come out of nowhere and hit us like a ton of bricks, stopping us in our tracks. These moments are true gifts, for they grab our attention in a powerful way and often lead to profound experiences and action that change our lives. We have the opportunity to make change daily for the benefit of our selves and for others but we often don't jump.

Our minds aren't always open or compelled to follow that inner voice or yearning, which is precisely why the notion of surprise, discovery and new experiences translates to action more often! We need something big, flashy, new or emotionally compelling to pull us out of the routine or box we live in. Once our attention is captivated and inspired, change can occur. The ability to recognize that such occurrences happen for a reason and to translate them to action is how positive change occurs. The expression, 'striking while the iron is hot,' is exactly the concept you must hold in your mind. Take action on an opportunity while the conditions are favorable and avoid waiting. Your likelihood of accomplishing your goal increases exponentially as there is a guiding force within you fueling your motivation to act and chase the outcome.

Generally speaking, our goals are self-driven, self-guided and self-profiting. However, the pathway to obtaining perpetual Joy in life is best achieved through the act of giving. Even in the daily moments we discover small bursts of Joy in offering a helping hand. Holding the door open for another, making eye contact, smiling, assisting someone in need, or simply saying "hello" are all great examples. A deeper sense of the word Joy is materialized when giving becomes personal.

> *"In everything I did, I showed you that by this kind of hard work we must help the weak, remembering the words the Lord Jesus himself said: 'It is more blessed to give than to receive.'"* (Acts 20:35, The New International Version).
>
> *"You are never too old to set another goal or to dream a new dream"* (Lewis). **– C.S. Lewis**

Over the course of this book you will embark on a personal journey unlike many others. It is a roadmap designed to reconnect you with the people and experiences that bring great Joy to your life. The beauty of this process is that it can be accomplished at any stage in life and will guarantee the delivery of the following:

Rediscovery of yourself and recognition of what brings great Joy to your life

A soul cleanse: A release of thoughts and feelings that will expose your authentic self

The gift of gratitude: Discovering that giving is in fact better than receiving

Learning to be present and re-committing to quality relationships

Reciprocity

This is a workbook, one that should demand journaling, doodling, dog ears, highlighting, underlining and "aha" moments galore! So grab that pen, highlighter and journal and let's dive in!

My son says pictures in chapter books make the story that much better. I agree, and in an effort to spur creative thought and inspiration throughout your journey, sketches will greet you at the start of each chapter heading. Onward!

CHAPTER THREE

DISCOVERING JOY: WHAT IT IS AND HOW TO FIND IT

THIS IS JOY

"Joy is the simplest form of gratitude"
(Barth).
– Karl Barth

It was my 37th birthday, and instead of gift cards, flowers, or jewelry my husband gave me a letter. This wasn't an ordinary letter but rather his expression of gratitude for me and our relationship. 15 years of Christmas, birthday and anniversary gifts had gone by, each special and meaningful, but all tangible. This letter was anything but tangible. In fact, I don't think I had ever seen or heard my husband express his feelings or appreciation for me in this way ever before, not while we dated, not on our wedding day, and not on any day thereafter. Sure, he had told me that he loved me and had showered me with compliments over the years, but this was different. This was the pure raw state of his emotions, an outpouring of his affections and inner-most thoughts onto paper. I felt bigger than life on that day and more appreciative of my relationship with my husband and the person he was because of the expression of gratitude he gave me. I also realized that the fact he hadn't verbally said each of those sentiments to me personally did not matter. In fact, there was something more powerful and sacred about hearing his voice through paper. Very specific, deep rooted feelings and gratitude can prove challenging to deliver face-to-face. In the peace and privacy of your own thoughts, these deep feelings come to life more easily through the solitude of pen and paper.

Sheer gratitude for the people in our lives is often not shared. We hear the expressions "thank you" and "thankful for" at Thanksgiving time, but specific statements are usually left unsaid. Rather, there is a shared expectation of known gratitude between two people. We neglect to recognize the remarkable impact that verbalizing these sentiments can have. The sheer power of a compliment and expression of deep appreciation for another can lift someone up and drive a deeper connection in a valued relationship. This is what that letter did for me and continues to do one year later. This is the gift that I will treasure throughout my lifetime, the gift I longed to receive but didn't know that I needed. Something sparked inside of me that day. What was this feeling? How could I manifest it, preserve it and replicate it? In that moment a quest began. A quest for what? That was the unknown. I knew that this moment and feeling were bigger than just a one-time occurrence. In fact, it took me months to connect the dots and deliver on what I believe today is the one of the greatest personal discoveries of my life. Through great reflection, thought and vision I set out on a journey that has had enormous impact on the way in which I lead my life, the manner in which I interact with others, my intentional commitment to the close relationships in my life and the art of being present.

CHAPTER FOUR

SOURCES OF JOY: IDENTIFYING THE PEOPLE IN YOUR LIFE RESPONSIBLE FOR YOUR JOY

> *"We tend to forget that happiness doesn't come as a result of getting something we don't have, but rather of recognizing and appreciating what we do have"* (Koeing).
> **Fredrick Koeing**

The sounds of bees were buzzing around me and the smell of wildflowers was in the air. A light warm breeze bushed my skin as I walked into church that beautiful Sunday morning. I often marvel at life's ability to imprint moments in our lives with such incredible clarity and purpose. This was one of those moments, God's way of telling me that on this day a profound change would occur. A discovery, purpose and great journey were about to take shape. That Spring Sunday in March I was meant to receive a message that would center my journey with great purpose and value for the lives of others. Cal Jernigan, Lead Pastor of Central Christian Church, was reading from Philippians Chapter 4 in the Bible and made this statement: *"Our quest for Joy is through the expression of gratitude. Joy is an emotion of delight and elation. It is contagious. Never keep your joy to yourself. It is meant to be shared."*

You know that feeling, the one you get when a smile stretches across your face, so big, so bright that you begin to feel aches behind your ears and a tingling from head to toe? Your heart is soaring, body temp is rising and you have an acute awareness of the blood pumping through your veins. You are experiencing the highest of natural highs that exist, a euphoric sense of enchantment. This represents the deepest physical and emotional response to happiness there is. People, relationships, experiences, life lessons, spiritual connections and memories deliver these endorphin-packed one-of-a-kind surges of happiness unlike anything else. That incredible moment in church helped me decide to make it my mission to help spread that kind of emotion.

There is a video on YouTube, "Baby Cries When Mom Sings" (Silva, 2013). It showcases the raw emotion of Joy transferring between a mother and a child as she sings to her baby girl. The facial expressions, tears and body language of the baby demonstrate the magnitude of Joy moving through her as she receives the outpouring of love from her mother. It is one of the best visual demonstrations of Joy in its pure physical form that I have seen. Milestone moments in our lives, like the first time you said "I love you" to a boyfriend or girlfriend, or the day you stood center stage accepting your degree or major award, gift us this remarkable feeling. The moment your significant other proposed to you; your best friend's speech at your wedding; the day your child was born …there are thousands of these moments that literally take our breath away and rock the very center of our core. They are peppered throughout our lives and are what give us the air to breath, will to live and inspiration to move forward. In many ways they are like a drug -- a good drug that far exceeds the impact of any other. We live for this drug, as we should. It propels the best version of who we are as human beings and keeps us hungry for more. This *is* Joy.

Understanding the raw elements and emotion of Joy is the first step in rediscovering what really makes you happy. Allowing yourself to recognize what has brought or continues to bring you Joy in life will further allow you to open doorways to your heart and soul. The most treasured moments in your life are stored within you, carefully hidden away inside a keepsake box, ready to call upon. You are the decision maker of what you hold on to. You are the key holder and have full control of opening the box that leads to the Joy in your life.

JOY: A very glad feeling; happiness; delight (Webster's New World Dictionary and Thesaurus, 1996).

Joy represents a source of deep delight and is traditionally not tied to something tangible. For example, the experience of deep delight or Joy is not associated with the purchase of a new car, house or wardrobe. Rather, Joy is something more deeply rooted, at the core of who you are. It lives among your morals, core values and most valued relationships. Often we get happiness confused with Joy. We spend our days and nights thinking about all of the "things" that we think will make us happy. If only I could make more money…If only I had that new car…If only my house was bigger, then I would be happy. Treating ourselves to new tangible goods is a part of healthy living so long as "want" doesn't far exceed "need," but it is not Joy. These purchase experiences and acquisitions have a shelf life. They are not anchored to our souls or tied to the heart strings of our very being. From the beginning we have been writing our stories and filling our memory banks with a collection of people and experiences. Our buckets have been filled with Joy time and time again through the many deposits made by others along the way. We owe much of our lives and growth as human beings to these people, yet our glasses appear half empty. We've been conditioned to believe that happiness is dependent on circumstances and tangible assets which we know is not accurate. It is an advertiser's dream! We have been brainwashed into believing that we need more gadgets, the newest technology, trendy clothes and cars. Competition is high, we are vulnerable and these dang people on the commercials look so incredibly happy with their purchase! This must be the key to happiness -- or so we think. Sure, the thrill is real and it feels darn good. But then it dissipates and we are left searching for the next big thing to fill our buckets momentarily. All the while, the people who pour into us eternally are sitting on the sidelines just waiting.

What fills your bucket daily, monthly or yearly? Let's brainstorm the many ways in which you experience Joy. Open up that journal, grab a blank sheet of paper or feel free to write in your book!

When was the last time you experienced extreme happiness? How did it make you feel?

Where, what and with whom, did you experience such Joy?

When did the major milestones in your life occur? Who was by your side?

Where and what experiences make you most happy?

Who is responsible for providing consistent happiness in your life?

Who has challenged you, inspired you and had great influence on your life?

Categorize your sources of Joy into: Things, Experiences and People

Tally up your categories and take note of which of the three represents your largest source of Joy.

When asked what brings people great Joy in life, the majority of people respond with, "the people." Does your list reflect the same findings?

Now that being said, these people represent a special group of intimate relationships that we deem high in value to us personally. They have had large impact on our lives in one way or another. They have cared for us unconditionally and have taught us critical lessons in life that we now include in our personal inventory. When asked about these people, we feel protective and appreciative in a way that exceeds our relationships with others. These people have challenged us, inspired us and have frankly helped shape our very being. It is through this group of special people, relationships and experiences that we find the most Joy in life.

CHAPTER FIVE

GETTING PERSONAL: RELEASING THOUGHTS AND FEELINGS THAT EXPOSE YOUR AUTHENTIC SELF

"In life, you will realize there is a role for everyone you meet. Some will test you, some will use you, some will love you, and some will teach you. But the ones who are truly important are the ones who bring out the best in you. They are the rare and amazing people who remind you why it's worth it." **– Unknown**

This chapter will be dedicated to discovery and reflection. We previously brainstormed what brings us Joy in life. We will work to expand that list by dedicating quality thought and time into writing down the people and experiences in our lives that have truly had the most profound impact on us both personally and professionally. It is easy to get caught up in writing down names of various people who have come and gone in our lives with marginal influence. Try to stay focused and committed to identifying the people who have played a significant role in your life's story.

As your life unfolds before your eyes and you tap into that keepsake box, your mind will be flooded with faces, memories, conversations, feelings, torn relationships, etc. The current status of your relationship with these people is not what matters. In fact, you will find that as you move through this process that time is not on your side. Months and even years have gone by and some of these once highly valued relationships have been brushed aside. Some have been lost purely due to the circumstances of life. Jobs, distance, family, school and growth have attributed to this lost connection. In other situations, intentional separation has occurred. A disagreement, difference of opinions, argument or other circumstance might be the cause of a stalled relationship. Use these tips to spur thought, purpose and certainty as you sort through these relationships.

Repeat to yourself: There is a reason why this person continues to come into my mind. At some point in my life, they have bestowed great value to me as a person, regardless of lost contact or current relationship wellness.

Stay honest with yourself. Dig deep and identify every person who needs to be on the list.

Family, colleague, mentor, friend...there are no exclusions to the roles of people in your life who have had the most impact on you. If they have brought tremendous meaning to your life, write them down.

You may be looking at your list and thinking one of two things..."Man, this list is long!" And, you may be right. This process will require that you refine your list carefully by looking at it through the following lens: In what ways am I thankful to this person for having influenced my life? In what specific ways have they added great value to the person I am today?

If you cannot imagine writing a letter to a person and answering these questions thoughtfully, then remove them from your list. This is not to say that there aren't hundreds of people responsible for having had an influence on your experiences, but Joy is about discovering the people and moments that have played larger roles in the rendition of life. Some relationships simply haven't had enough time or opportunity to reach this level of impact. As life progresses, your list can expand and you will know with confidence who is in need of hearing from you and when.

On the flip side, some of you might be thinking, "Hmmm...my list seems too small." This can happen when you do not allow your heart and mind to open fully. This is a Rediscovery of You process, one that will require you to think back through the years and carefully comb through the many people and experiences of your life. You will need to be honest with yourself and refrain from discarding a person from your list simply because your relationship is on rocky ground or you question their feelings for you.

There is no magic number when it comes to tallying up the people you wish to express gratitude to. Our lives are filled with unique experiences and people. Whether you have 5, 15, 32 or 100 people to express gratitude to, your list is your own and will look unlike any other.

What if some of the people you identify have passed away?

How can gratitude be expressed to small children?

These are good questions and lead to meaningful outcomes of this project. One of the most beautiful aspects of identifying those who bring you great Joy is being able to write down the many ways in which they have impacted your life. You have your own story with each person and there will be shared memories of love, laughter, inspiration, etc. The process of writing these experiences, feelings and sentiments down on paper is in itself joyful. Your memories will come to life over pen and paper and magic will unfold into your sentences as you feverishly type away on that keyboard. One of the driving forces of this project is to seize the opportunity to express gratitude now rather than later; sharing this expression to those who mean the most to you while they are alive and well is essential for both the giver and the receiver. Delaying your expression only hinders relationship growth. Unfortunately, regret exists when we lose the opportunity to express meaningful gratitude to a person of great value while they are still with us.

However, you must tell yourself that the moment is not lost. Writing to those who have since passed away is a critical piece in this journey. It is both healing and joyful to write to a lost soul whom you carry close to your heart. Their spirit will be alive within you as you write, guiding you and hanging onto every word. As if they were sitting right beside you, more alive than ever before, their presence will be known. You will finally give the gift of gratitude and there will be a sense of peace and closure that follows. You may learn that other people in your life who cared for this person will find Joy through your sentiments. There will be a shared appreciation for your Joy. And through the words and sentences of your expression, this letter may prove to be one of life's greatest gifts for a person who shares your love for this lost soul.

Children can be handled in two separate ways:

You can choose to keep your notes simple and appropriate for their age.

Or, you can hold onto your letter until they are mature enough to comprehend all you want to share.

A meaningful way of postponing a message of this nature is to open up an email account in your child's name. It will allow you to document significant moments, achievements or feelings with your child over the year, and it will be the greatest gift to give your child on his or her 18th birthday. The email account and password will unlock years of moments chronicled by Mom and Dad -- a gift unparalleled by any other.

As your gratitude list takes shape, use this statement as a filter to finalize the names you have identified.

I am the person I am today because of the lessons I have learned and experiences that I have shared with these people.

This vetting process will take some time and only once you are confident with the list of names that you have gathered will you be ready to advance to the writing phase. Expression of gratitude for what people bring to your life is evergreen, meaning it is fluid and ever-changing. Months or even years down the road you may realize that there was a person you had forgotten about. This happens because our memory is like a card catalogue. We have experiences and people filed away and it takes a flashback or something new but familiar to trigger that person, time or place. Sometimes these Joy triggers are the best experience of all. They transport you back in time where you can vividly recall the feelings, atmosphere and details of that single moment in time, and you can't help but smile. These are some of life's most beautiful treasures. Additionally, as you move into the future new people and experiences will imprint on your life. These people will enrich our lives and become part of our story. They will share new life experiences with us, teach us lessons, help us grow, drive purpose and gift us love, expanding our gratitude quest along the way. This is the beauty of life; each phase is a new adventure. Embrace it, lean in and recognize the beauty of what is yet to come.

"Appreciation is a wonderful thing. It makes what is excellent in others belong to us as well" (Voltaire). **– Voltaire**

CHAPTER SIX

THE POWER OF A COMPLIMENT: THE GREATEST GIFT

> *"Gratitude is the fairest blossom which springs from the soul"* (Beecher).
> **– Henry Ward Beecher**

We all remember the movie Jerry Maguire and Tom Cruise's famous scene with Renee Zellweger. Tongue-tied and trying his best to express just what she meant to him, he comes out with, "You complete me" (Jerry Maguire). A one liner that summed it all up...or so we think. We have an easier time being expressive and succinct with what we mean to say when it is written, not stated. Emotions are in check and we can recall specifics. The "wow" behind expressing gratitude lies in the detail, the elaborate description of your feelings, or the way in which you describe the characteristics of a person. This ability to depict the precise features of a moment or an occasion with a specific person is what breathes life between two people over paper. Be honest, be raw, be you. Unveiling your authentic self and thoughts over paper is what unleashes the power of your voice and emotion. Sincerity matters and the purpose here is to lay it all out there. Don't hold anything back. Share your inner thoughts with those who need them most. There is beauty in all things sincere.

> *"Be honest, brutally honest. That is what's*
> *going to maintain relationships"* (Hill).
> **– Lauryn Hill**

Questions to provoke the details of gratitude:

What is it that you have gained or learned from your parents?

What tough lesson did you learn from a leader that has transformed the way in which you lead today?

In what ways do you appreciate your best friend?

How have the people in your life brought you great meaning and purpose?

Through the support of another, how have you conquered the toughest of challenges?

This group of individuals has moved you to your core and it is your job to unearth the details and bring them to life over paper. This goes beyond the standard one liners that we have a tendency to fall victim to in the moment of expression: "I love you." "You are amazing." "What would I do without you?" "You have taught me so much." "Thank you." "You're really great." "I really like working with you." "You mean the world to me."

The expression of gratitude must be detailed in order to drive impact. This will be the single most powerful gift of Joy that you can give. It is a compliment on steroids. It will reinforce certainty in place of assumptions. It will strengthen the awareness of known talents and assure them that your relationship served great purpose. The emotional gift of being acknowledged goes beyond any other. Being recognized for making a difference or adding value in another person's life is the highest compliment there is. It means that we matter, and it means we are significant to someone, somewhere, in this great big world.

In my son's elementary classroom of 1st-3rd graders, it is a standard practice to create and gift a compliment book to each child on his or her birthday. The children are educated about what constitutes a compliment and asked to create a page with a written compliment and drawing to be given to the birthday boy or girl. These are then bound in a book and given to the child on his or her birthday to read. Not only is this a brilliant means for teaching children about the value of compliments, but it encourages them to practice kindness to others routinely. This act of expression is so very special and evokes an incredible emotional response from a person of any age. I look forward to watching my son read his compliment book created by his classmates each year. There is no greater gift.

Can you imagine receiving such a gift each year from your family and friends? How about once in your lifetime? This is what we will work to achieve. The greatest gift we could give to the people who mean the most: a one-page letter filled with compliments all about them.

> *"Feeling gratitude and not expressing it is like wrapping a present and not giving it"* (Brault)
> **– Robert Brault**

Chapter Seven

Letters of Gratitude: Unleashing Your Inner John Hancock

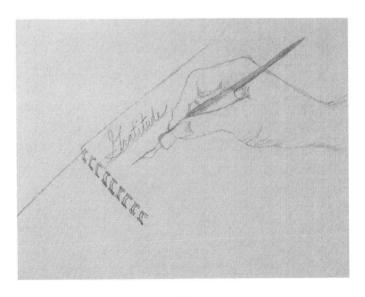

> *"Gratitude unlocks the fullness of life. It turns what we have into enough, and more. It turns denial into acceptance, chaos to order, confusion to clarity. It can turn a meal into a feast, a house into a home, a stranger into a friend. Gratitude makes sense of our past, brings peace for today, and creates a vision for tomorrow"* (Beattie).
> – Melody Beattie

Welcome to the writing phase! This is where the magic begins to unfold -- the place where we begin drafting letters of gratitude. This is the roll-up-your-sleeves, let's-get-down-to-business section of the book. Let's dive into the key components needed to bring this project to life.

Key Components:
Tackling a goal and finding the ease in it all
Not a writer? No problem!
What to say to the person you haven't spoken to in ages
Addressing confrontation and forgiveness
Postmark, email or instant messenger: Gathering contacts
Finding the time to accomplish

Tackling a new goal and finding the ease in it all:

"This goal is too hard. I couldn't possibly do this." These are normal feelings and thoughts that prevent us from embracing change, trying something new, facing conflict or overcoming the fear of rejection. Yes, some of this process will be new, emotional, hard work, but it will come with an ease far beyond what you imagine. It is certainly not a race, but rather a marathon -- a marathon that is paced by you and you only. The reward will be worth the work and come easier than you might think.

Before we begin, I would like for you to close your eyes and take a deep breath. Open your mind and imagine that you just set sail on a sailboat alone in the ocean for the first time. The day is picture perfect and you've completed your sailing course with flying colors. The ocean is waltzing and the wind is serenading you. A gust of wind has filled your sails and the boat is propelled at magnificent speed. The ocean is guiding you along and energy is flowing effortlessly through you. At first you are breathing heavily with nervous energy, then softly with ease and confidence. Your emotions take hold. You are as free as a bird and your smile takes over. Your smile can only get bigger through the tears that form as you feel Joy encompass you. You are at the helm of your boat and she is soaring! Now open your eyes. This breeze and sense of gliding is what you will feel as you put pen to paper. For that moment in time you are connected with the very person you are writing to and a surge of energy will drive your thoughts to paper effortlessly.

Writing to the most important people in your life is not difficult. Your words, sentences and experiences will fly from pen to page. You will find that you cannot write as quickly as your mind is creating. There is an instinctive connection taking place between your heart, mind and emotions. You've just unlocked the door to your keepsake box and you are on fire! You are suddenly able to recall everything that you love and appreciate about the person you are writing to. Recalling the experiences you shared or lessons you learned as vividly as the day they occurred, you can describe every detail and they are translating to paper effortlessly. This emotional connection will provide you the energy to do your work. It won't take long to comprehend why the writing phase is the most beautiful of all. Fasten your seatbelt and enjoy the ride.

No writer? No problem!

While this book is not designed to give you the verbiage needed to compose your letters, it will serve as a framework to get you started. These are simple letters and not novels in length. You are the artist and your words must be your own. Remember, these people are among the closest to you and will want to hear your voice through your writing. As a society we have gotten off the beaten path of mailing letters, writing in script or even writing at all. We have abbreviated words that we had no business abbreviating and have replaced conversations with text messages or emails almost entirely. The beauty and delight that comes with receiving a letter is sadly rarer than ever. We rarely even send a simple note of genuine interest to one another anymore. We live utterly dependent on our interactions with one another via social media posts or text threads. This is yet another reason why this form of gratitude expression is so effective. We are more isolated than ever before and in need of human connection. Let this be a driving force for you as you work to write your letters of gratitude, and use these prompts to get started.

Opening:
I've been on a personal journey writing to the people in my life who have had the most profound impact on me both personally and professionally. You are most definitely one of these people. I would like to share with you how you have added value to my life...

Middle:
I appreciate you for the person you are because...
I value our relationship for these reasons...
I have learned this from you...
You have influenced my life in these ways...
The experience we shared has changed my life because...

I wouldn't be the person I am today without you in my life because…

Close:
I am thankful for the conversations / experiences / memories that we have shared…
I am grateful to have you in my life…
You have brought Joy to my life and I am forever grateful…

To wordsmith is an art all its own. A letter of gratitude looks and feels much like a glorified greeting card. However, this greeting card will be treasured more than any Hallmark card ever could. There are countless ways to express thanks, appreciation and gratitude. Some of you will fall in love with the art and craft of designing each unique expression of gratitude. Others, however, may initially struggle with finding the right words to express such a heartfelt letter. Igniting the poet within you can be accomplished at TheGreetingCardPoet.com. Here you will find beautiful and colorful ways to begin the process of expression (http://www.thegreetingcardpoet.com).

What to say to the person you haven't spoken to in ages:

The great thing about close or integral relationships is that time does not diminish value. Even that professor back in college who had a profound impact on your learning or career path will find value and Joy in hearing how he or she influenced your life. We each have a good friend whom we've lost touch with over the years, a person who to this very day, consumes our thoughts and has left an empty feeling in our hearts. The combination of lost time and lack of effort often lead to a feeling of despair. You may begin to wonder and ask yourself these questions:

Do they remember me?
Do they remember the times that we shared?
Was our relationship important?
Do they think of me now?

The process of reaching out with a sincere note of gratitude changes everything. You will learn that the answer to the questions above is almost always a resounding "Yes!" It is quite amazing to watch a relationship that has been distanced for long periods of time ignite almost instantaneously through the expression of gratitude. It is as if lost time simply washes away and two people are reconnected with the very same bond they once shared long ago. These reactions are by far the most rewarding. You will be astounded with the sheer excitement of a response. In many ways it feels serendipitous, as if they were waiting and longing for you to reach out all along. What a beautiful feeling! Remember, time has no real impact on relationships of value. This act of expression squashes any fear, uncertainty or previous assumptions. It will debunk the myth that lost time is harmful to relationships. This is one of the greatest outcomes of this project. The elation you will experience as a result of reconnecting with a person that has great meaning to your life is beyond measurable value. It will physically and emotionally lift away the burdens, questions, fears, sadness and guilt associated with allowing these relationships to drift away. As human beings, we allow time and fear to build a wall that seems impossible to climb over. We then shock ourselves by learning that something simple can be done to overcome and achieve. This expression of gratitude is one of the simplest acts that someone can take in an effort to knock down that wall. It will take no time at all to resolve one relationship at a time. You will gain back the time in your days, weeks, months and years that you once sacrificed to fear, uncertainty and doubt with the people in your life. You will instead dedicate regained time to positive thoughts and actions. Get ready to "wow" yourself and the people in your life, who have frankly waited and longed to hear from you as many times as you have thought of them. Time has no impact, as the connection we share between heart and mind is unbreakable. We are simply reigniting the flame that once burned with the passion of communication.

Addressing confrontation and forgiveness:

As we learned above, we dedicate real time to thinking about the lost or tarnished relationships in our lives. These thoughts and fears eat at the very heart of our being and consume our minds with waste. This waste, in literal form, robs minutes, hours, days, weeks and years from our lives. It can leave us feeling hopeless and depressed. The relationships that we once held closest to our hearts and are now tarnished for one reason or another, are among the most important for rediscovering Joy. As the old saying goes, 'Say it before it is too late.' This is an excellent guiding principle for this phase of the journey, as it will prove to be the hardest. It's no surprise as to why it will be the most challenging of all. We are human beings and we flat out struggle with confrontation. We don't like to forgive and we most certainly don't like taking accountability for our actions -- that is, when these actions are not reflective of our better selves. Now, this is a big category of lost relationships which we'll need to be break down.

"To Err is human; to forgive, divine" (Pope).
– Alexander Pope

It's easier to forget than forgive. Or is it? At first glance, forgetting seems like the easier path. But in reality, over time the exact opposite proves to be true. The truth of the matter is, we simply never forget. Instead, we spend more and more time thinking and stewing over the details. We contemplate alternative outcomes, judge actions and gossip to others for years over the situation. In many ways, these confrontations with relationships of value can consume our lives. It can alter who we are as individuals and give others a false perception of the person we are and what matters most to us. It can be utterly exhausting for both you and the people in your life.

"You are what you think." One could argue that this famous expression is an outcome of overcoming confrontation. It begs the questions: Who are you? What would others say? Is there something or someone in your life that gives you daily heartburn? If the answer is yes, then learning to forgive or confront may be the answer. A letter of gratitude is a safe haven for expressing harbored feelings, honesty and hope for reconciliation. A letter doesn't judge and allows your mind to speak freely and release your thoughts once and for all. An honest expression of your feelings to another with the intent to forgive is in fact, the greatest gift you could give to yourself. When you air out your dirty laundry and come clean with a person of significance, the details of what caused the confrontation begin to fade. It is a regular psychological response to releasing the details that have consumed your mind day in and day out. Your mind shifts to the peace that follows conflict resolution. Euphoria and a sense of relief calm your mind knowing that what is done is done. Life can go on.

Taking accountability, and seeking forgiveness:

> *"It's one of the greatest gifts you can give yourself, to forgive. Forgive everybody."*
> (Angelou). **– Maya Angelou**

"I was wrong." "I'm sorry." "Can you forgive me?" Why is it that these statements are among the hardest to say and even harder...to *mean*? You would think that we were asked to climb Mount Everest, jump off a cliff, share a den with the lions or swim with sharks. Nope. Just take accountability. We choose to sacrifice some of our most valued relationships with the people we love the most due to these phrases. We will go our entire lives avoiding these statements and the people they are associated with like the plague. Why would we risk such a thing? Why would we give up the very things that bring us great meaning and Joy in life? The answer: Because it is easier.

As human beings we find the word "sorry" derogatory. It is a word that we associate with loss, failure, wrong, guilt and shame. It attacks the lifeline of who we are, chips away at our confidence and erodes our happiness. So we choose not to say it. Instead, we hold it in until we become the literal meaning of these words -- guilty, failure and sorry. Saying "sorry" or seeking forgiveness from the people in our lives that mean the most is a game changer at any time. It can resolve and establish harmony at any phase of life. A confrontation that has caused strife in a relationship must be restored before it is too late. Whether this is with your spouse, child, parent, grandparent, friend, colleague or spiritual connection, no one should miss the opportunity to seek forgiveness. Life is not intended to be spent apart from the people you were meant to be with. The weight of this guilt or lost relationship is among the heaviest that we carry around. Some people will carry it throughout their lives, never choosing to let go, and will literally take it to their grave. This is not the answer. If we allow this to happen, then we have all lost. Seeking forgiveness or writing to reconcile a relationship over paper could, in fact, save your life and that of another. We tend to neglect the weight that these tarnished relationships have on our well being and need to do something about it. Absolutely nothing is worth throwing away a relationship of great value -- nothing. It is highly likely that the other party is feeling the very same way. They are just as scared as you and it all comes down to making the first move. Make the first move? No way, no how, not me! But in life there are countless moments and opportunities that will in fact require one person in a relationship to go first.

"Will you be my friend?"
"Will you go out with me?"
"I love you."
"Will you marry me?"

"Can you forgive me?"

Be the first to make the move; you will not regret it. You have everything to gain and nothing to lose. Let your letter of gratitude be the vehicle you need to restore the important relationships in your life. You will pick up living where you left off and stop wondering, "If only I had said the things I meant to say before it was too late." As the Nike brand says, "Just Do It" (Nike).

> *"Forgiveness is the final form of love"* (Niebuhr). **–Reinhold Niebuhr**

CHAPTER EIGHT

GETTING IN TOUCH: POSTMARK, EMAIL OR INSTANT MESSENGER

> *"Appreciation can make a day, even change a life. Your willingness to put it into words is all that is necessary"* (Cousins).
> **– Margaret Cousins**

Thanks to social media and the internet, this is one of the easiest times in recent history to be able to tackle an endeavor like ours. However, before we sell ourselves on the convenience and time-saving benefits of electronic communication, let's take a look at the power of a handwritten note.

Post Marked Mail:

"Even though technology has changed the way we communicate, receiving a handwritten, personalized note still touches our emotions in a way instant communication tools can only dream about" (Hallmark Business Connections, 2016). A handwritten or typed letter sent via traditional mail will trump any other in value. Receiving a letter via mail is a beauty and a delight in itself. It is a tradition, one of the first modes of communication and is still considered the most sincere. With the introduction of cell phones and the internet, communication via mail has fallen to all time lows. Why? Most would argue that it takes too much time. Our lives have become so incredibly busy that even communicating has become a chore, a chore which we have micromanaged to the most minimalist form: abbreviation. My daughter has renamed our world "busyland," not to be confused with Disneyland because to be honest, it's rather stressful to manage. Even for a child, from the outside looking in, life is incredibly busy! So before you jump to typing your gratitude letters, consider this. When was the last time that you received a handwritten note of significance from someone important? How did it make you feel? Could you feel emotion pouring through their words simply by looking at their handwriting? Could you actually envision them sitting there writing that card to you? Perhaps you could see their smile, body posture, or the motion of their hand as it conveyed the most sincere thoughts of their heart and mind. This vision alone brings more Joy to your heart than the words themselves. An individual's handwriting is theirs and theirs alone. It is as effective as face-to-face communication and in many ways can carry an added layer of honesty and openness that simply doesn't always come across when speaking person-to-person. It is everything personal, sincere and authentic. Much of this persona, emotion and authenticity lose potency when the letter is downgraded to type. Type masks the stroke of our pen and hides the raw emotion of who we are. Handwritten letters are, hands down, the most special. Like me, many of you probably have a box or drawer in your home safeguarding your most treasured handwritten letters. Time stands still as you reread these letters, reuniting you with the moment you first laid eyes on them. The specifics of that moment -- the day, your age, the message, your feelings – everything is right there in front of you. A handwritten letter holds remarkable value and sacred emotion throughout a lifetime. In fact, these treasures are often gifted to future generations. The ability to touch a handwritten letter in the script of an ancestor is incredibly powerful. The heart and mind can connect over paper even better than over a photo. Consider these benefits when choosing a method of draft for your expression of gratitude. That being said, typed letters can be as effective and are better than no letter at all. This option of course requires that you have current mailing addresses for your recipients.

Email:

In 1999 Meg Ryan and Tom Hanks romanticized the concept of opening your email box to hear three delightful words, "You've got mail" (You've Got Mail). And that's exactly what it did. It established a private connection through a dial-up experience on your computer with another person anywhere in the world. The pure awe of being able to send and receive such personal communication in a matter of minutes was astounding on its own. Email quickly became the most efficient form of communication, serving a high value purpose in the lives of all people. Email has changed dramatically over the course of the last 20 years and the essence of 'you've got mail' doesn't always give us the warm fuzzies as it once did all those years ago. Like never receiving a letter in the mail, most of us rarely receive a thoughtful note from someone personal in a letter format. In fact, the vast majority of email these days is representative of junk mail, sales pitches, tasks or forwarded threads of communication trending from one person to another. It is even rare to receive a simple "Hi, how are you doing?" note via email from someone you know or care about. In many ways, email is simply becoming a record keeping system for communication. This paper trail process for storing information or conversation is transaction heavy and constitutes low personal value. You have an opportunity to send your letter of gratitude via email and give someone the warm fuzzies all over again. Bring back the Meg Ryan and Tom Hanks magic of dialing in to hear, "You've got mail."

A special note to consider when using email is that most users have security set at high levels to ward off spam and junk mail. You will want to inform the recipient via text or other form of simple messenger systems that an email may be waiting in their junk mail from you. This is the one drawback to using email and unfortunately can interfere with the recipient receiving your letter. This may in turn cause you to move to other forms of communication. How will you know? It is estimated with 100% certainty that you will receive a response from each person who receives their letter. A letter of gratitude will never go unnoticed and its perceived value will always warrant a response.

Facebook Messenger / Social Media Messaging:

While social media in many ways has hindered "quality" communication with others, it has opened a gateway to communicating one-on-one through its instant messaging tools and resources. Like me, many of you have 10 or more friends and connections on social media platforms, such as Facebook, Instagram, Twitter or Snapchat. You can find just about anyone you ever knew through the search function on one of these accounts: your elementary school best friend, the girl who bullied you in the 5th grade, the first boy you had a crush on, your favorite boss, your mentor in college, the person you studied abroad with or your cousin that you haven't seen in ages. "Today, more than 3 billion people use the internet on a regular basis and more than 2 billion are active social media users. Interestingly, teens are not the only ones hooked to the web, and Gen Xers aren't the oldest ones on Facebook or Instagram. Baby Boomers, who in the U.S. have a population of roughly 80 million, are growing in online number every day" (Jafrey, 2018). A simple Google search will help you find the person you are looking for associated with one of these social media power houses. Facebook Messenger is an excellent option for writing your letters of gratitude in a format that looks and feels much like receiving a personal letter via email. The same feature exists in LinkedIn for any of your connections with former colleagues, leaders or professionals. There is no limit to the number of characters written, and formatting comes across much like a letter and less like an informal text message which is entirely the point. The greatest gift that these social media platforms have given to us is the ability to find one another and maintain a relationship, further proving that messenger tools provide a great means for the crafting and sending of gratitude letters.

You now have all that you need in order to track down contact information and send your letters of gratitude. There should be no barrier to achieving your goal of expressing gratitude to the most important people, the people who have had the largest personal or professional impact on you, in your life. In a world of reading impersonal newsfeeds, where the average person spends an estimated 5 hours of his or her day, receiving something of real value out of the blue can be earth shattering.

CHAPTER NINE

FINDING TIME: ACCOMPLISHING A GOAL OF GREAT IMPORTANCE

> *"We are all in the gutter, but some of us are looking at the stars"* (Wilde). **– Oscar Wilde**

Time or lack thereof is really a matter of perspective. Time is often our largest excuse for just about everything in life. 'If only I had more time.' Time is 100% dependent upon choice -- your choice. While yes, life has changed since the 1950s and the smorgasbord of options available for how to spend time has stretched far beyond what it once was, choice remains. Living situations have changed, commutes to work have increased, job expectations look different and a higher percentage of households represent two income earners. Where time waste occurs most often lies in "extra curricular" time. We have literally flooded this space with ways in which to consume our time. Simply watching one TV show wasn't enough, so we invented binge watching, the ability to watch an entire season in one night! Reality TV and the lives of others for some reason captivate our attention and the Internet is a literal black hole of distractions. We watch people unwrap and play with toys on YouTube and spend hours scanning endless social media feeds with news bits, ideas and personal life updates. We are hooked! We want to be in the know now and aware of what's happening in everyone's lives. Society has put competition into just about everything and to be honest, none of us has enough time to keep up at this pace. This is our reality, one that requires making good choices about what deserves our time and attention. There are ways to find balance in these spaces without going to either end of the extreme. You certainly don't need to shut out the world and live as a cave man, but you must not allow yourself to be swept away. Be purposeful and in control of how you spend your time always. You must make a plan and intentionally set aside time to accomplish the things that are important to you in life. Listen to the profound advice offered by wise philosopher Ferris Bueller, "Life moves pretty fast. If you don't stop and look around once in a while, you could miss it" (Ferris Bueller's Day Off).

When was the last time you received a personal note from someone you really cared about? When was the last time you had an in depth conversation about life with a good friend or family member? So, you can only imagine what it would feel like to receive a personal letter of gratitude from someone of importance to you. In addition to what we've gained thus far, this process will aid in restoring deeper levels of one-on-one communication. Many of the conversations that we have today with just about everyone in our lives convene at a surface level. We have busy schedules, text messaging and social media feeds to thank for that. Who has time for a "real" conversation anymore? In reality, these series of quick, abbreviated exchanges with people wear us out! They have become yet another job, to do list item, and societal expectation. Real conversations with people, either over the phone, in person over coffee or via personal letters do not need to take place daily, weekly or even monthly for that matter. You may go 6 months or more before you have quality time to sit down and really engage with someone who matters to you in your life. And guess what? It is okay. You gain far more from the "real" conversation than you do from text messaging, snap chatting, instant messaging and reading one another's social media posts for the entire year. This is true because real human engagement occurs at deeper levels of connection. There are physical and emotional outcomes of these engagements that generate endorphins. These endorphins motivate, and provide a sense of value, love and thoughtfulness that simply cannot be achieved at surface level discussions. This is also where the pressures, expectations and judgments fall aside. You are able to expose your true self and effortlessly enjoy the conversation as you are intended to do. There is much mutual benefit here and we all need a lot more of this in our lives. So, schedule it. It is proven that if you do not focus, set a goal or structure a plan for something it will often fall off your radar, making you that much more susceptible to the dangers of wasteful time consumption. Set your own pace. There is no time limit or competition with this goal. The way in which you prioritize when, where and who you start your journey with will be up to you. Your goals for how often you write and complete your letters will also be set by you. The key here, like with any other goal, is that you create it, set a timeline and work to achieve it.

"Being thankful not only shows good manners, but a simple expression of thankfulness can go a long way in relationships and communication with others. It not only enhances our own lives, but makes other people feel appreciated" (Whyte).
– Daniella Whyte

CHAPTER TEN

THE STARTING LINE: KNOWING WHEN AND WHERE TO BEGIN

> *"What you get by achieving your goals is not as important as what you become by achieving your goals"* (Thoreau).
> **- Henry David Thoreau**

Make a commitment
Pick a day to start your first letter and write it down. Make it specific. Decide who will be the first recipient of a letter of gratitude from you. You may have someone in mind at this very moment, either due to an active situation occurring in life or simply because your heart is speaking to you. Grab your pen and write his or her name down. Your journey and commitment starts now.

Celebrate your accomplishment
You must celebrate the accomplishment of anything you set your mind to do! Acknowledging the small wins is what propels you forward to achieve more. A spoonful of achievement goes a long way in the grander scope of a large goal. Each finished letter will inspire you to write another, and sometimes two or three! Ride the wave of inspiration and act on what motivates you to move forward.

Re-Commit & Finish
Make another commitment and write it down immediately following the previous accomplished task. Decide the rhythm of your commitments to writing (1x

per day/week/month). In full disclosure, it took me the better part of a year to complete my letters. Some required a moment of opportunity or clarity to complete, while others I wrote in batches because I was inspired to do so. Resist the urge to procrastinate. These letters do not require much from you and they pack a real punch for everyone involved. No timer is set and whether you finish in 3 months, 6 months, 1 year or even 2, what matters is that you cross that finish line. None of us can predict the future, nor can we use the past to justify waiting to act on something. Really challenge yourself to live in the present and take every opportunity to act on what matters most now. None of us wants to live with regrets and this thought alone should motivate you to complete your journey.

Like anything new, the hardest part of your journey will be the beginning -- actually committing to start. It won't take long to realize just how effortless this process really is. You must begin in order to discover. It may take something urgent, pressing and BIG to motivate the when, where and most importantly "who" that kicks off your journey.

Something BIG like cancer will do it; it did for me. I was compelled to write my first letter when I learned that my stepfather was battling for his life against pancreatic cancer. As a family we came together and planned a trip to spend time with him within a couple of months. The visit was wonderful and much needed; however, it didn't give me the opportunity to express my deepest thoughts, feelings and expression of gratitude. I just couldn't express all of the things that I really wanted to say in that moment. My emotions were in full control and I lacked the ability to formulate thoughts. Like the colors and rows of a Rubix Cube circling, my mind was unable to bring order to expression. And so I said goodbye with everything left unsaid. On that three-hour flight home, in deep thought and reflection, I came to realize that my opportunity had not been lost. Within 24 hours of returning home, I began to write. Finding the things that I needed to say was easiest of all. They were in my heart all along and it took this ugly word called cancer to literally kick my butt into gear. Suddenly all of the things that I felt for this person were there right in front of me. So were these questions:

Does he know how much he means to me?

Have I ever really told him?

My grip on that pen was tight and full of purpose. As if my very own hand was possessed, it forced thoughts to paper with intense vigor. My mind was spewing thoughts as a volcano spews lava. My body could not keep up. As the mind unleashed, emotions took flight. Ups, downs, twists, turns, free falls and release -- one heck of a roller coaster ride! Then, as fast as the ride commenced, it was over. I was out of breath, clammy, exhausted and relieved. All of the things that I had ever hoped to say and needed to say were there in front of me, ready to be shared.

SENT. Just like that, in an instant my letter was on its way. I shared my most intimate feelings with this person and bared my soul; I felt ecstatic! Nervous energy began to build as I thought...

What will he think?

What will he say?

Will this letter bring significant meaning to him?

It was in his response that this project and purpose took flight, further proving the original hypothesis: Your quest for Joy is through the expression of gratitude.

"Thank you from the bottom of my heart for everything you have said. It brings me the greatest Joy in reading your letter. You will always be my little girl whom I helped and love. Your success in life brings me the greatest Joy and so does the fact that you have included me as a part of it."

BAM! The wind was literally knocked out of me. The surge of Joy and elation that spread from my fingertips to my toes was unlike anything I had ever experienced. The sheer appreciation for honesty and gratitude gifted in return for the act of such expression reaffirmed my mission and intent to write my next letter. I flat out refused to allow something as ugly as cancer to initiate the expression of gratitude to the other people in my life who meant the very most to me. I wanted to share with them now. This surge of energy and purpose helped me expand on my vision and lay out a plan. I spent hours and even days determining who had impacted my life the most. As we've discussed thus far, they weren't all a bed of roses. In fact, some of the most meaningful letters took fear, forgiveness and accountability head on. These were difficult to start but became easier once the wound was exposed and resolved. The momentum gained throughout the process was due to the reciprocity of Joy. My wildest hopes and dreams could never have predicted the gifts that would unfold as a result of this project.

I am awestruck and baffled by life's teachings and limitless possibility. I am in more control of being present than I have ever been before. Frankly, it has become my mission of sorts. The relationships in my life are at the pinnacle peak of what health and happiness should look like. They are engaging, reciprocal, value-driven and bonded at a level of happiness best described as joyful. This is where I will choose to keep them forever. Never again will I allow time, busy schedules, social media, life distractions or tangible assets come between the Joy that fills my cup and that of others daily.

CHAPTER ELEVEN

TRUST IN TIMING: SEIZING MOMENTS OF OPPORTUNITY

> *"Hold the vision, trust the process.*
> **–Unknown**

Timing is everything. Through faith and trust, a moment of opportunity will unfold before your very eyes. When such an opportunity presents itself, you must jump at it. You may not know how or why, but there is absolutely a reason for its timing. The concept of 'everything happens for a reason' has proved true to me. With my vision and goals as my guide, taking notice of the doors opening around me proves easy. The number of opportunities becomes mind blowing. Regardless of your faith, it is hard to deny such opportunity and timing. A spiritual force within me is guiding me to move, see and act on more possibilities than ever before.

> *"Gratitude bestows reverence, allowing us to encounter everyday epiphanies, those transcendent moments of awe that change forever how we experience life and the world"* (Milton).
> **– John Milton**

Fear, uncertainty and love initiated the drafting of the letter to my stepfather. The timing was evident, the door was open and the opportunity cost of not sharing my feelings was high. These circumstances supported the great need to act quickly. Noticeable moments of opportunity are not all created equal. Some will in fact be driven by fear and uncertainty, while others will be tied to beautiful happenings in life: birthdays, anniversaries, Mothers' Day, Fathers' Day, Christmas or any day at all really. Some days you will just be inspired. Something inside of you will grab your attention and spur a memory and for that very reason you will write. Some mornings I wake with vivid memories of my dreams. Or, my first thought of the day may be about a particular person. I may not know the reasons why that person comes into my mind, but I have learned that they are there intentionally. This project has taught me to act on these moments and reach out, if even to say "hello," rather than allowing the moment to pass. Coincidentally, each and every time I have done this a purpose unfolds. The receiver was in need of hearing a supportive voice for some rhyme or reason. This has altered the way I interpret the needs of others and the simple daily ways in which I can serve and gift my support to the people I care about most. This project has paved ways for many positive life outcomes, one of which is finding ways to habitually serve and enrich the lives of others. It is simple to maintain and is mutually beneficial for everyone involved. Acting on these moments requires little time and effort. They are intentional random acts of kindness packaged in prayer, thoughtfulness, conversation, support, or a smile. This is real life change -- positive life change that can be committed to and sustained across a lifetime.

When people ask me about my parents it takes me more than 2 minutes to share my story. Like several modern day family trees, mothers, stepmothers, fathers, stepfathers, aunts, uncles and grandparents play active parental roles. I consider it a blessing to have had the gift of six parental figures in my life. Each has imprinted on me in different ways and helped shape the woman and mother I am today. On my expression of gratitude list you will see mother, father, stepmother, stepfather, grandpa and grandma. These are my parents. You too will likely have your parents at the top of your list and writing to them out of the gate may seem like the easy answer. Don't be surprised when you sit down and put pen to paper that the words don't pour out so easily. These relationships that share the deepest roots of time, experiences and emotion can prove most challenging. Let me explain.

My dad's letter carried weight of spiritual depth, love and time that simply left me lost in my own mind, not knowing where to begin. For that reason, his letter was one of my last. It took a clear moment of opportunity to present itself before I was able to tackle such an endeavor. One evening over the phone my brother mentioned that my dad was having heart problems. I remember thinking, "How? Why? When did this start?" I had spoken to him recently and he hadn't shared this news. So what did I do? Well I phoned my dad of course. Unlike most of our conversations, Dad spent time telling me about his childhood and fondest memories with his mom, dad and uncle. He rarely spoke about his family but for a moment he allowed himself to express emotion that has probably been bottled up inside for quite some time. He told me about how wonderful his dad was and how much he wished that I could have known him, because he was great with kids. He told me about how he strived to be just like his dad, willing to teach and experience the wonders of life and adventure with his own kids while he was young and able to do so. And then he said, "You love your parents but you never really tell them all the reasons why you just love them so much until they are gone. It is only then that not a day goes by that you wish you could tell them just how much you love them." In the long breathless pause following that comment on the phone, my heart stopped. I took a deep breath and said, "Dad, you know that I love you right?" But for some reason, the simple fact of stating "I love you" over the phone in that moment did not carry the weight or meaning that those powerful words should deliver. How could those words feel so empty and meaningless? But they did. It was then that my dad told me about the heart surgery he was scheduled to have in 2 days. I knew instantly that I had to write my letter of gratitude and show my dad just what those words "I love you" have meant throughout my life. I spent three hours that night writing my Dad's letter. I poured my heart out and said everything I needed to say and then some. It cost me $35 to send that letter to my Dad overnight via UPS and it was the best money I ever spent. My dad's heart surgery was a success and I couldn't be happier knowing that he was able to read his letter the evening before heading to the hospital. My dad said, "Your letter made me cry." We didn't talk much more about it, because really there is nothing more to say. When two people exchange raw honesty and emotion at its truest intent, peace and calm is what follows. A mutual understanding, respect and strengthened bond form.

In life everything has purpose and meaning. Sometimes it takes years, even decades, to connect the dots. My dad was my teacher, coach, and greatest fan in new experiences. He taught me how to camp, downhill ski, water ski, dive, fish and explore. It was the 80s and Nike's "Just Do It" campaign was in full swing. I had a Nike "Just Do It" (https://www.nike.com) tank top that I wore often and it quickly became my dad's motto for just about everything, especially when encouraging me to jump! We would laugh and joke, but in all seriousness, that expression became my motto in life. There are countless experiences in my life both personal and professional where "Just Do It" provided me with the surge of confidence needed to accomplish anything my heart desired. Hearing my dad's voice on the phone that night was nostalgic. It took 30 years, but the quote that bonded us together from the beginning had finally come full circle. "Just Do It." Because there is nothing more important than being able to express gratitude to the people in your life you care deeply for.

The right time to send your letter is often something that you cannot plan or foresee. In my experience these moments arise out of nowhere as if summoned by God Himself. A moment will present itself and your instincts will grab hold and tell you what to do. I have learned to trust in time, knowing full well that my moment will arise and my instincts will surge and compel me to seize the opportunity to send a letter of gratitude. The key here is to act fast when it does. I believe that these moments present themselves as triggers and reminders to take action when it is most appropriate in an effort to drive ultimate impact. Never doubt your instincts and do not shove these critical moments to the side. They happen for a reason and will be your motivation to complete your mission.

CHAPTER TWELVE

THE BOOMERANG EFFECT: RECIPROCITY AT ITS FINEST

> *"At times our own light goes out and is rekindled by a spark from another person. Each of us has cause to think with deep gratitude of those who have lighted the flame within us"* (Schweitzer).
> **–Albert Schweitzer**

In the late 1970s, a popular children's show titled "Boomerang" captivated the television sets of many Seattle preschoolers. Marni Nixon, a Broadway star with an incredible voice, mesmerized viewers with the opening song, "A boomerang, a boomerang, what does it do? It comes back to you. It comes back to you. A boomerang a boomerang, bing bong bang that's boomerang" (Keen 1975). While the song goes on and on, it's this very essence of what a boomerang does that makes our own journey take flight. Like a boomerang, reciprocity gives and then gives again.

> *"It is an absolute human certainty that no one can know his own beauty or perceive a sense of his own worth until it has been reflected back to him in the mirror of another loving, caring human being"* (Powell).
> **– John Joeseph Powell**

The range of emotions that returned in response to each letter was beyond expectation. Tears, Joy, appreciation, elation, expressed gratitude in return, shock, and expressions of need and timeliness all came back to me. Below are just a few of the sentiments I received.

"Wow!" The word most frequently expressed at the beginning of each response. The impact of receiving a letter of expressed gratitude goes beyond any basic human expectation. The surprise of being reconnected to a person of great meaning out of the blue, in a meaningful way is somewhat earth shattering. In simple form, receiving a personal note from someone in a sea of daily impersonal interactions can manifest extreme delight and emotional happiness.

> "This letter means so much to me and is something I will keep forever. Honestly, it was the nicest thing ever written to me in MY LIFE, so thank YOU."

> "The letter was overwhelming and brought tears to my eyes."

> "Your letter was an unexpected gift and probably the nicest thing anyone has said to me in a long time."

Brutal honesty. As human beings, we simply do not expect brutal honesty or outpourings of authenticity from one another. It is refreshing and triggers a response of comfort in being able to express the very same thing in return.

"I never knew you felt that way. I am overwhelmed just taking it all in."

"I keep re-reading. I cannot get enough of what you just said."

"I loved hearing all of your words."

"I appreciate everything that you said."

"Thank you for your kind words."

"Beautifully honest."

The feeling is mutual. The expression of gratitude in return is common. This is unexpected delight of reciprocity at its finest. Be prepared to be blown away with an honest expression of gratitude in return. It's the gift that comes back to you tenfold.

"You have no idea how much you meant to me."
"This is the most wonderful gift I've received in a long time."

"I do not have words to describe my gratitude for all the kindness you shared."

"I chose to write you in response to your letter because it would be difficult to find all the words on a phone call to describe how I feel and all that I would want to say."

The timeliness of your letter. The need for a human connection is real. Often an unintended consequence of your letter is to buoy a person when they need it most.

"It came at such an uncertain time in my life."
"I cannot express the absolute perfection in the timing of your note!"

"What excited me about your timely letter was for me it was a quickening in my spirit reminding me that some special people, like you, will ALWAYS be in my life!"

A true revelation of this process was seeing the expression of a needed human connection. In a society where we are connected to each other at a moment's notice in the palm of our hand, one can be blinded to the fact that we are actually more disconnected than ever before. Some of us are thrown into forced human interactions daily through our jobs and family needs. However, this is not the case for everyone. Think for a moment, how many of the people on your list have someone active in their lives that "need" them? Do they have a daily human connection? The answer for many is no. "Only around half of Americans (53%) have meaningful, in-person social interactions, such as having an extended conversation with a friend or spending quality time with family, on a daily basis" (Polack, 2018). What about your own interactions? Do they have a balanced representation of relationships of value to you? Or are you merely in the throws of managing human interactions that lie at a surface level in life? Have you found that your own family has lost the ability to communicate? The sad truth is that the answer to these questions is often yes, bringing even further urgency to reestablishing the quality in relationships. We need to turn back time and relearn what it means and takes to communicate.

On a grander scale, the breakdown of real communications has led to an unhealthy human society. It's not hard to connect the dots between increased suicide, depression and the mass obsession with selfies. When stripped back to the core, each is a result of a lost human connection. We are lonely. As human beings we need each other. We were meant to be influencing one another, loving on each other, serving together, and discovering as one. It is a natural effect that when we don't have these basic needs met, we begin to invent ways in which to receive them. We become overtly obsessive with presenting and proving our self-worth. We become focused on showcasing why we are the best, better than others, and in need of extra attention. Our actions may appear selfish, offensive, out of the ordinary, and borderline disrespectful. This is because we are truly not thinking clearly. We have reached a human connection low. Our tank is empty and the only way to fill it is to self-consume and often this is done on extreme levels. These levels of self-infatuation attract judgment and criticism, which only makes the situation worse. It is saddening to see that such a situation has grown to epic proportions and a pandemic caused by loneliness is resulting in the devastation of basic human wellness.

We were made for more and each of us has the opportunity to accomplish great things in this life. Adding value to others and to this beautiful world is the responsibility of all of us. With loneliness as a barrier to reaching our potential, we must recognize the issues and overcome them by reaching out to someone in need. Many of the people in our own lives appear to be just fine on the outside, when in fact they too are in need of a human connection. Social media allows us to put on a good face and display a life full of happiness and contentment when inside many of us are lonely. As you read this chapter, I hope that you are beginning to picture the faces of those who mean the most to you. Who might be in need of that human connection within your circle of family and friends? When was the last time you spoke in person, or better yet, saw one another face-to-face? "Nearly half of Americans report sometimes or always feeling alone (46%)" (Polack, 2018). You can imagine my own surprise when I discovered that approximately 50% of the people closest to me expressed need for my letter of gratitude. 50% of the people I care for most were navigating through uncharted times in their own lives, in need of a real connection. What about you? There is a lesson to be learned in everything. In this we relearn that we have an obligation to one another. Now get up, get started and make real change in the lives of those who mean the most to you. They need you, and you need them.

> *"The deepest principle in human nature is the craving to be appreciated"* (James).
> **– William James**

CHAPTER THIRTEEN

LEARNING TO BE PRESENT: MOVING RELATIONSHIPS FROM SURVIVING TO THRIVING

> *"There are only two ways to live your life. One is as though nothing is a miracle. The other is as though everything is a miracle"*
> (Einstein 1941).
> **– Albert Einstein**

If you would have asked me one year ago what life-changing outcomes could result from this project, my response would not come close in comparison to what it has actually rendered. There is a final outcome that I've titled the 'Re-Commitment' phase. As we've discussed, this experience re-connects you with the people you care for most on a raw level, a level that feels like a new beginning. It is everything real, sincere, true, beautiful, motivating, and full of purpose and potential. The energy that burns as a result of this rekindled connection manufactures a drive to re-commit to a quality relationship. You've overcome the hardest step in the process: reaching out and expressing sincerity and gratitude. Why put the book back up on the shelf? No way! This is not a one-and-done activity. This experience and your natural instincts will drive you to take the next step. Re-committing to a quality relationship will require and demand being "present" in every meaning of the word. You will experience a new sense of responsibility and pride at being present in the lives of others, giving yourself in your truest form without doubt or lack of confidence. It simply comes down to doing what's right: making a positive difference in the lives of others because you care and you can. You will find yourself re-committing to countless phone conversations, random acts of kindness, intentional plans to interact face-to-face and much, much more. This ball that you are rolling will now take on speeds that defy reason. The light inside of you will not have a moment to go out. It will look for random possibilities to be present with just about anyone. You will constantly be searching for people in need, for the ability to add value to others, for the chance to offer a helping hand or to simply bring a smile to someone's face if even for that one moment in time. These once distant relationships with the people who you call most important will be dusted off, removed from the top shelf of that book case, opened up and read daily.

> *"It takes 21 days to develop a habit"*
> (Maltz 1960). **– Maxwell Maltz**

I recently had to re-learn how to drink water. I know this sounds funny, but I was simply not getting enough water and my doctor explained that in an effort to change my hydration habits, that I would need to start by retraining my brain. The goal that I was given was to consume 8 ounces of water each hour for every waking hour of the day. I was to record how much I drank each hour on a chart each day. To begin the process, I had to set a timer. Can you believe how fast an hour goes by? It seemed like I had just had my water and there it was again…beep, beep, beep. My brain was clearly not used to reminding my body that I needed water hourly. Once the first week was up, I decided to progress without the use of the timer. As you can expect, I would do okay for the first few hours, relying on my memory to check the clock for water hourly. Then something would distract me. I would get wrapped up in work or with the kids and suddenly three or more hours had gone by without a reminder from my brain. It took concentrated effort over the course of the last two weeks to re-train my brain into drinking water and guess what…it worked! 21 days later, I not only had an inner clock reminder to drink water hourly, but my body started to show signs of thirst hourly as well! This was an eye-opening experience for me. Re-learning to communicate with others on a routine basis will also require a habit change. Over the years our brains have been trained to communicate in different ways. This project will require our brains to head back to the gym for some heavy lifting. With consistent training and execution a new habit will form. Grab a planner and commit to daily, weekly or monthly goals that will require a consistent repetition of communication with the people in your life. Schedule conversation dates and set an alarm on your phone to remind you. 21 days of consistent execution of this process will get you back in the saddle! You will remember just how great it feels to have real, fruitful communication with the people in your life and, best of all, you will crave more! As we've discussed earlier, active connections with other human beings are essential for both mental and physical health. They're as essential as drinking water.

> *"Fill your life with experiences, not things. Have stories to tell, not stuff to show."* – **Unknown**

You may find that a re-commitment to some relationships will spur a deeper need for connection. This is where joyful experiences meet joyful relationships. When time, energy and savings are put forth to bring these two components together, relationships climb to greater heights. Experiencing life, discovering the world and doing so with someone you have a deeply sacred relationship with can help you reach peaks of Joy. Dedicating time to plan that trip home to see family, accomplishing a bucket life item with a friend, or reconnecting with a spouse on a vacation away from children, jobs and life pressures can be among the best soul food there is to be had! There is no greater way to renew one's self or build upon relationships with others than an active adventure or exploration. Stop putting off that trip, ignoring your inner voice and allowing excuses to prevent you from doing what you know to be important. Make a plan, commit to a date, surrender one source of wasteful spending and instead, save what you need in order to make this dream a reality.

> *"True wealth is not measured in money or status or power. It is measured in the legacy we leave behind for those we love and those we inspire"* (Chavez). – **Cesar Chavez**

Reciprocity will begin to take on new heights with the people in your life. Joy is contagious and many will follow in your footsteps through the process of drafting letters of gratitude, bringing new meaning to the expression, 'paying it forward.' Watching others experience Joy, discover their potential, move relationships from surviving to thriving, and regain the act of being present in life is powerful. Your bucket of Joy will be overflowing. More importantly, you will notice a substantial change in yourself-- a change that is everything positive, progressive, confident, and intentional. It is through deeply meaningful experiences like these that we become reacquainted with ourselves by recognizing what's truly important in our lives, expressing gratitude to those who bring us great Joy, recommitting to being present with others and living out our dreams.

CLOSING THOUGHTS

I believe it was intentional for me to be in church on that day one year ago listening to Pastor Cal Jernigan state, "*Our quest for Joy is through the expression of gratitude.*" And now I've found conclusion at the very same place. As I sat in church this past Sunday and listened openly to Cal's big idea below I thought, "This is it. I was meant to be here on this day to receive this powerful message."

> "*Every incredible experience in life begins with an invitation.*" **– Lead Pastor, Cal Jernigan**

He went on to say, "It only takes 5 seconds of courage to say 'yes.' The five seconds that follow an invitation are the most important seconds of your life. All relationships and new beginnings begin with an invitation."

For this very reason today, you have been presented with this book and an invitation to embark on a personal journey that will change your life and that of the relationships you have with others forever. The time has come, and in the five seconds that follow this moment is your opportunity to say yes. All it takes is a little courage.

As Helen Keller once said, *"Life is either a daring adventure or nothing at all"* (Keller).

Bibliography

Arlen, H., Harburg, Y. (1939). Over the Rainbow. The Wizzard of Oz [Motion Picture]. Culver City, CA: MGM Metro Goldwyn Mayer.

Fleming, V., Vidor, K., Cukor, G., Thorpe, R., Taurog, N. (Director). LeRoy, M. (Producer). (1939). The Wizard of Oz [Motion picture]. Culver City, CA: MGM Metro Goldwyn Mayer.

Marshall, R. (2018). Mary Poppins Returns [Motion Picture]. Burbank, CA: Walt Disney Pictures.

Crocker, J., Oliver, M., Nuer, N. (2009). Self-Image Goals and Compassionate Goals: Costs and Benefits, Self and Identity. Retrieved on June 5, 2018 from https://www.tandfonline.com/doi/full/10.1080/15298860802505160?scroll=top&needAccess=true.

Silva, Joao Edgar. "Baby Cries When Mom Sings." You-Tube. YouTube, 5 March 2013. Web, 18 August 2018.

Agnes, M. (Ed.) (1996). Webster's Mew World Dictionary and Thesaurus. Simon and Schuster, Inc. New York.

Hughes, J. (Director). Jacobson, T. (Producer). (1986). Ferris Bueller's Day Off [Motion picture]. Los Angeles, CA: Paramount Pictures.

Schwedop, K. (Director). Groce, B. (Producer). (1975). Boomerang [Television series]. Seattle, WA: KOMO.

Keen, S. (1975). Boomerang. Boomerang [Television series]. Seattle, WA: KOMO.

Ephron, N. (Director). (1998). You've Got Mail [Motion Picture]. Burbank, CA: Warner Bros.

Http://www.thegreetingcardpoet.com

Crowe, C. (Director). (1996). Jerry Maguire [Motion Picture]. Culver City, CA: TriStar Pictures.

Hallmark Business Connections. (2016). The Power of a Handwritten Note. Hallmark Business Connections Blog. Retrieved October 2, 2018, from https://www.hallmarkbusinessconnections.com/the-power-of-a-handwritten-note/.

Jafrey, I. (2018). Social Media Matters to Baby Boomers. Forbes Technology Council. Retrieved July 7, 2018 from https://www.google.com/amp/s/www.forbes.com/sites/forbestechcouncil/2018/03/06/social-media-matters-for-baby-boomers/amp/.

https://nike.com Polack, E. (2018). New Cigna Study Reveals Lonliness at Epidemic Levels in America. Cigna. Retrieved September 9, 2018 from https://www.cigna.com/newsroom/news-releases/2018/new-cigna-study-reveals-lonliness-at-epidemic-levels-in-america.

Powell, J. (1974). The Secret of Staying in Love. Cincinnati: RCL Benziger.

Jane. 20 Quotes to Inspire Gratitude. Habits for Wellbeing. Retrieved November 1, 2018, from https://www.habitsforwellbeing.com/20-quotes-to-inspire-gratitude/.

Mordini, S. 20 Quotes to Get You Fired Up About Gratitude. Mind Body Green. Retrieved September 28, 2018, from https://www.google.com/amp/s/amp.mindbodygreen.com/articles/20-quotes-to-get-you-fired-up-about-gratitude—6877.

C. Jernigan, personal communication, March 19, 2017).

C. Jernigan, personal communication, May 6, 2018).

About the Author

Malia Sperling is a wife, mother of 2 and passionate people leader. Through an intentional quest for life balance, this revolutionary thinker has completed a deep dive of life priorities, discovering that authenticity is in many ways a key ingredient to *self* awareness, confidence, purpose, success, joy and balance. She has been blessed with an adventurous career in business, where she learned the value of being truly authentic. In a world of corporate ladders and executive personalities, learning to navigate through politics and games is as vital as learning the job itself. Hard work, transparency, integrity and passion are what Malia would describe as her keys to success and commitment to self. With a fierce passion for people development, Malia's greatest joy as a leader is learning about the genuine attributes of people, their God-given talents and the ways in which they use them to influence others and business. She lives to see people grow and achieve!

An honest reflection of life priorities, their level of importance and timing is what has driven Malia to focus on finding joy in life. Understanding what centers your joy in life will ultimately lead to a re-discovery of self, priorities and aspirations that promotes authenticity and purpose.

As a leader, speaker and coach, Malia is passionate about supporting others along their authenticity journey. "This *is* Joy" is a starting point for self-discovery, reflection and a re-commitment to being present with the people and experiences in life that matter most.

CONNECT WITH MALIA

If you are looking for a little more joy or authenticity in your life, I would be delighted to connect with you daily via my blog at www.theauthenticeffect.com or via Instagram @theauthenticeffect.

I would love to hear and engage with you about your gratitude journey, "aha" moments and the many blessings that have manifested in your life! Our life explorations are meant to be exploited and shared. It is through this experience that the benefits of reciprocity will come to life.

Additionally, if you are looking for a more intimate discussion about your personal and/or professional journey, I gladly offer coaching services that support the recognition, development and application of authenticity in life. It is never too late to stop for a moment, shed the layers and re-evaluate what makes you tick and whether or not you are allocating time appropriately to serve and promote growth in each meaningful area in life. A deep look and evaluation of life priorities is good for everyone at several stages in life. Through the adoption of intentional planning and execution, joyful living is entirely possible.

"Inspiration and motivation that stems from a place of authentic joy and purpose is what leads to profound accomplishments in life."

–Malia Sperling

Urgent Plea!

Thank You For Reading My Book!

I really appreciate all of your feedback, and I love hearing what you have to say.

I need your input to make the next version of this book and my future books even better.

Please leave me a helpful review on Amazon letting me know what you thought of the book.

Thank you so much!
~ Malia Sperling

Made in the USA
San Bernardino, CA
10 July 2019